Celebrating your year

1973

a very special year for

D1726663

A message from the author:

Welcome to the year 1973.

I trust you will enjoy this fascinating romp down memory lane.

And when you have reached the end of the book, please join me in the battle against AI generated copy-cat books and fake reviews.

Details are at the back of the book.

Best regards,
Bernard Bradforsand-Tyler.

This book was written by Bernard Bradforsand-Tyler as part of *A Time Traveler's Guide* series of books.

This is a work of nonfiction. No names have been changed, no events have been fabricated. The content of this book is provided as a source of information for the reader, however it is not meant as a substitute for direct expert opinion. Although the author has made every effort to ensure that the information in this book is correct at time of printing, and while this publication is designed to provide accurate information in regard to the subject matters covered, the author assumes no responsibility for errors, inaccuracies, omissions, or any other inconsistencies herein and hereby disclaims any liability to any party for any loss, damage, or disruption caused by errors or omissions.

All images contained herein are reproduced with the following permissions:
- Images included in the public domain.
- Images obtained under creative commons license.
- Images included under fair use terms.
- Images reproduced with owner's permission.

All image attributions and source credits are provided at the back of the book. All images are the property of their respective owners and are protected under international copyright laws.

First printed in 2022 in the USA (ISBN 978-1-922676-08-5).
Self-published by B. Bradforsand-Tyler.

ESPIONAGE AT WATERGATE HEARINGS

OIL EMBARGO– PLUNGE INTO CRISIS

Rocky Horror Show Shocker!

Flashback to 1973 a very special year

BOMBS EXPLODE IN LONDON

WAR IS OVER IN VIETNAM

ROE v. WADE LANDMARK RULING

KING wins Battle of the Sexes

Let's flashback to 1973, a very special year.

Was this the year you were born?

Was this the year you were married?

Whatever the reason, this book is a celebration of your year,

THE YEAR 1973.

Turn the pages to discover a book packed with fun-filled fabulous facts. We look at the people, the places, the politics and the pleasures that made 1973 unique and helped shape the world we know today.

So get your time-travel suit on, and enjoy this trip down memory lane, to rediscover what life was like, back in the year 1973.

This could be the tape deck you'll leave your great-grandson.

You want a tape deck that lasts? We'll give you a tape deck that lasts. And lasts.

It's the new Sony TC-377. Its three ferrite tape heads last up to 200 times longer than conventional tape heads.

It also has mixing controls that let you mix two sound sources. (For instance, your life story, narrated by you against background music.)

And a tape tension regulator to keep the tape traveling smoothly, without wow or flutter.

And a slant-front cabinet that can stand up, or lie flat.

And superb sound. Whatever weird instrument your great-grandson will be playing, the Sony TC-377 will capture it.

Isn't this better than a gold watch?

Sony.

Contents

1973 Family Life in the USA

Imagine if time-travel was a reality, and one fine morning you wake up to find yourself flashed back in time, back to the year 1973.

What would life be like for a typical family, in a typical town, somewhere in America?

1973 was an unsettling year for Americans, beginning with the collision of numerous seemingly disparate yet remarkable events, all crammed into four action-packed days in January. On 20th Jan, President Richard Nixon was inaugurated for a second term. Within days, his predecessor Lyndon B. Johnson suffered a heart attack and died. The same day, the supreme court delivered its landmark decision in the case of Roe v. Wade, declaring that the US Constitution provided pregnant women the right to an abortion. Over in Paris, American and North Korean delegates agreed on terms for a Peace Treaty, ending America's eight-year-long involvement in the Vietnam War.

Demonstrators in Washington, DC, demanding the impeachment of President Nixon following the Watergate hearings, 22nd Oct 1973.

By the end of the year, we were facing a four-fold increase in oil prices, a tripling of inflation, sky-rocketing unemployment, a crash on Wall Street, and the worst recession since the 1930s.

In the ten years to 1973, the US population had increased by 10% to 215.2 million.[1] Americans accounted for only 6% of the world's population, yet consumed a whopping 33% of the world's energy. The US economy accounted for a quarter of global production.

The Baby Boomers had become a large, vocal population of young adults. Birth rates and family sizes continued to fall, thanks to changing family values and readily available contraceptives.

Some of the 600,000 attendees at the *Summer Jam Rock Festival* at Watkins Glen, NY, July 1973.

The Loud Family starred in *An American Family* (PBS. Jan 1973) becoming the first reality TV family. Back, from left: Kevin, Grant, Delilah and Lance. Front, from left: Michele, Pat and Bill.

The hippie view of the world, with its emphasis on peace, love and nature, had focused our collective attention on the anti-war, anti-pollution, and anti-consumerism movements. The Watergate scandal and the rising cost of living and unemployment levels reinforced our rejection of our parents' old traditions and conservative values. Our distrust and disgust for authority and for the status quo increased further. African Americans, LGBT communities and environmentalists ramped up the fight for recognition and equality.

[1] worldometers.info/world-population/us-population/.

It's a new world...and the Mamiya/Sekor DTL is a vital part of it.

The new kind of photographer doesn't collect fancy cameras to impress friends. He or she takes pictures. Why have a few hundred thousand of these new photographers bought Mamiya/Sekor DTL cameras? Because its special dual metering system makes it easier to shoot in difficult light situations. Whether the sun is in front, back or to the side, flick the Creative Switch. Take a "spot" or an "averaging" reading and be sure of perfect exposures everytime. Priced right, with enough left over for an extra lens. See your dealer today. It's a great camera on any trip.

At the same time, the feminist movement had been gaining momentum. Women in greater numbers were achieving higher levels of education, increasing their confidence, and independence. Divorce rates were rising steeply. An estimated 50% of couples who married in 1973 would end up divorced in future years.[1]

Universities and colleges became breeding grounds for free-thinking, liberal theories. Students often shared accommodation, partly for convenience and cost savings, but also as an expression of a new way of living, cohabiting, exploring sexual freedoms and spiritual fulfillment.

In 1973 the median family income was $11,120 a year.[2] Unemployment stood at 5.2%, with GDP growth at 5.3%.[3]

Average costs in 1973 [4]	
New house	$27,866
New car	$3,930
Dishwasher	$220
Vacuum cleaner	$69
A gallon of gasoline	$0.36

[1] nationalaffairs.com/publications/detail/the-evolution-of-divorce.
[2] census.gov/library/publications/1973/demo/p60-90.html.
[3] thebalance.com/unemployment-rate-by-year-3305506.
[4] thepeoplehistory.com and mclib.info/reference/local- history-genealogy/historic-prices/.

Life in the United Kingdom

Now just imagine you flashed back to a town in 1973 England. Although not all doom and gloom, the United Kingdom had found itself slipping on the world stage as America and the USSR battled for domination.

The joyful, carefree optimism of England's Swinging Sixties could not last forever. The decade of the '70s was marred by continuous industrial strife. Power struggles between the government and the powerful trade unions peaked in 1973, and would plunge the country into darkness when Prime Minister Edward Heath declared a three-day work week to save electricity.

The sentiment on the streets had shifted from frivolity to revolution. This was echoed in the street fashion, music, arts and culture.

The "Troubles" in Northern Ireland had been raging for decades. Irish Nationalist campaigns became increasingly daring, spilling into the streets of cities across the UK as activists took to bombing commercial and political targets as far afield as central London.

Left and above: London street scenes from 1973.

The British feminist movement had a long-established history and continued to gain strength throughout the 1970s.

The newly formed Women's Liberation Movement quickly grew to become a national movement, with thousands of grassroots groups. Their list of equal rights demands included equal pay, equal education, and free contraception.

Women protestors, six-deep, stormed The Grill, a men's only pub in Aberdeen, Scotland, demanding to be served, 20th Apr 1973.

In 1973 the average age of marriage for women was 25, and the average age for the birth of their first child was 26.[1] The fertility rate was 2.0 births per woman, down from a peak of 2.9 in 1964.[2] The contraceptive pill (available since 1961) and the legalization of abortion in 1967 aided in this decline.

The Divorce Reform Act came into effect in 1971, allowing for divorce without reason and leading to a steep increase in divorce rates.

In the early '70s around 50% of families owned a car.[3] Within the larger cities, most people still relied on public transport.

The rate of car ownership had been steadily increasing in the years before 1973 (around 3% growth per year). However, this growth stagnated for the five years to follow as a result of the oil crisis and economic recession.

[1&2] ons.gov.uk/peoplepopulationandcommunity.
[3] ons.gov.uk/ons/rel/ghs/general-lifestyle-survey/2011/rpt-40-years.html.

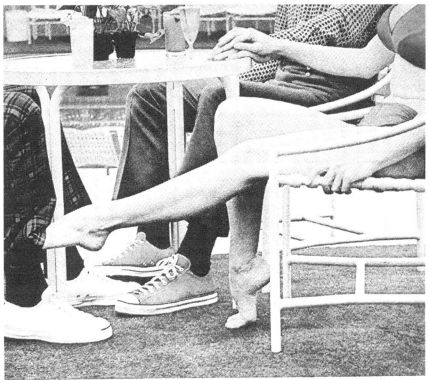
Converse Coach and Jack Purcell.

For guys who want to keep playing after the game is over.

Converse has built a reputation for making great athletic shoes for the greatest athletes in the world.

And that's the idea behind our Converse Coach and Jack Purcell. Great performers. But they look great, too.

A terrific all-around athletic shoe like Coach (right), that looks good enough to play the field off the field, too. And a great tennis shoe like Jack Purcell, that feels just as at home partying as playing tennis.

Two tough-playing, sharp-looking leisure time shoes from Converse. Because some guys are out to build a reputation for themselves.

Converse Coach and Jack Purcell.

By 1973, the UK was nearly half-way through repaying its post-war debt to America and Canada. The 20-year post-war building boom, which had kept cash flowing and unemployment low, was over.

Economic growth in the UK was only half that of Germany and Japan, with annual GDP having slipped from 2nd place in 1960 (behind only USA), to 5th place in 1973. Moreover, UK GDP per capita had fallen to 26th place in world rankings.[1]

By 1973, most of the former colonies of the United Kingdom had been granted independence. The cost for the UK to keep and defend them had proven too heavy a burden.

Across the nation, marches, protests, riots, industrial strife and strikes were increasing. Inflation (at 9.2%) was skyrocketing. The UK in 1973 was a country in decline. And this was just the beginning. The worse was yet to come.

The remainder of the decade would bring a mounting series of economic crises, industrial actions and major political battles.

Top: Police guide marchers in the UK's second *Gay Pride Rally and March*, from Embankment to Hyde Park, London, 1973.

Left: Engineering workers' strike at Tower Hill, London, 1st March 1973.

[1] nationmaster.com/ country-info/stats/Economy/GDP.

By the early '70s, the Baby Boomers were young adults. Everything about them was a break-away from their parents: their music, their fashion, their values, their personal and sexual freedoms. They were non-traditional, non-conformist, anti-authority, anti-consumerist, anti-war, politically active, experimental drug users, hippies, believers and disbelievers. Anything was possible. Everything was acceptable.

The "Back to the Land" movement and the rise of communal living in the late '60s and early '70s were lifestyle expressions of freedom of choice. Communes were anti-establishment and experimental, communes were whatever the inhabitants chose them to be. Up to 3000 communes existed in the USA during this period.[1]

In the state of Vermont, a haven for hippies, an estimated one third of young adults (below age 34) were living communally.[2]

[1&2] forbes.com/sites/russellflannery/2021/04/11/what-happened-to-americas- communes/?sh=7454bc05c577

Most communes encouraged co-ownership of possessions, collective chores and shared child-raising. For many, clothes, monogamy and drug usage were optional. By rejecting the 40-hour work week, many communards relied on food stamps, or temporary odd jobs to keep themselves nourished.

In rural areas communards practiced living off the land, setting up farms, building their own houses and selling handicrafts.

Myrtle Hill Farm, Vermont.

A geodesic dome house built at Myrtle Hill Farm, Vermont. Recalls one communard, "In 1971 a young man named Bernie Sanders visited Myrtle Hill Farm... Sanders' tendency to just sit around talking politics and avoid actual physical labor got him the boot."[1]

Communards at Hog Farm, California.

The rise of communal living in the late '60s and early '70s was worldwide. Although the vast majority only survived a few years, some communes continue to exist today.

[1] From *We Are As Gods: Back to the Land in the 1970s on the Quest for a New America* by Brian Doherty.

The 1973 Thunderbird.

In appearance, in appointments, it's a luxury car.

In ride and handling, it's distinctly Thunderbird.

The automobile that is known for ride and luxury has even more to offer this year.

Its suspension system has been refined and tuned to its steel-belted radial ply tires. Tires that are tested to give the average driver 40,000 miles of tread life in normal driving. Result: an extraordinarily smooth ride.

Some other special luxuries: cushioned front seats with twin center armrests. The comfortable efficiency of Thunderbird's power brakes and power steering. The classic look of its new optional Opera Window.

Experience it at your Ford Dealer's.

A unique luxury automobile   Thunderbird   Ford division

The new 1973 Thunderbird pictured above also includes as standard equipment new energy absorbing bumper guards, left hand remote control mirror and white sidewalls. Other equipment shown is optional.

Our Love Affair with Automobiles

Our love affair with automobiles began back in the early '50s, and by 1973 America's car addiction was unrivaled in the world. More than 101.4 million cars traveled our roads. Vehicle numbers had risen 48% during the preceding 10 years. Although automobile costs had risen markedly, so too had real wages, making cars increasingly affordable. The family car had become a necessity we could not survive without.

Traffic congestion in Atlanta in the early '70s.

Increased car ownership and the creation of the National Highway System gave us a new sense of freedom. Office commuters could live further out from city centers, in cleaner and more spacious suburban developments, and commute quickly and comfortably to work.

Rural areas faced a steady decline as the suburban population continued to rise. By the early 1970s, only 26% of the population remained in rural areas.

Catering to the suburban lifestyle, fully enclosed, air-conditioned shopping malls sprang up country-wide. A typical design saw one or two anchor stores with hundreds of smaller specialty shops, sitting within a vast expanse of carparks.

Valley View Center, Dallas, opened in August 1973.

Detroit was the car manufacturing powerhouse of America, where "the Big Three" (Ford, General Motors and Chrysler), produced the bulk of cars sold. Although still renowned for their gas-guzzling "muscle cars", pressure from imports and domestic demand for more compact, fuel-efficient cars led to a general downsizing. Compact and sub-compact car sales grew, increasing markedly after the Arab Oil Embargo in late 1973.

Chrysler Plymouth Gold Duster, 1973.

American muscle cars increasingly battled to maintain relevance and dominance. These high-performance coupes with large, powerful V-8 engines and rear-wheel drive had been designed to satisfy our desire for power above all else. But the introduction of the Clean Air Act of 1970 forced automakers to drastically reduce emission pollutants. Clean air equipment became the new focus, robbing engines of much of their raw power and performance.

GM Oldsmobile Cutlass Salon, 1973.

AMC Hornet Hatchback, 1973.

"The styling coup of '73"

American auto makers responded to the stricter federal requirements, and to the increased competition from imports, by creating compact, more fuel-efficient car models. However poor design, inadequate engineering and manufacturing led to a stream of disasters, damaging the customer experience.

Five car-producing countries dominated the industry in 1973: Japan, Germany, England, and France, with America in the top spot. Japan's meteoric rise into this elite group had been particularly aggressive, and their cars stood poised to dominate the world markets.

Japanese cars were reliable, affordable, compact, efficient and popular, quickly making Toyota, Nissan, Mitsubishi, Mazda, Datsun, and Honda the export market leaders. Japanese car exports increased nearly 200-fold in the ten years to 1973.

Presenting Datsun 610. Considering the luxury, its economy is all the more remarkable.

Own a Datsun Original.

Porsche 914 coupe, 1973.

As we became more aware of the hidden dangers and impracticalities inherent in American car designs, European and Japanese cars were seen as more reliable, safer and more fuel-efficient.

Introducing the 1973 Beetle:

Re-introducing the 1972 price: $1999

In the early '70s, the Volkswagen's Beetle became the world's best-selling car. However, competition from Japanese cars saw Beetle sales decline in 1973. Volkswagen responded with a new generation of water-cooled, front-wheel drive cars.

Introducing Buick Century. Priced under $3700.

It's the steal of the Century.

We've taken big Buick features and put them in a new smaller size.

Some examples:

AccuDrive. Buick-built for stable handling even on bumpy roads.

Dual-Rate Body Mounts. To isolate car from road vibration. For smooth, quiet ride.

Solenoid-Actuated Throttle Stop. For quick, sure engine shut-off.

Time-Modulated Choke. For quick starts in cold weather.

Air Injection Reactor. For emission control and smooth, smooth idling.

Front Disc Brakes. For confident straight-line stops.

Computer-Selected Chassis Springs. For superb ride and handling. Based on weight of the car and equipment you order.

Padded instrument panel, padded head restraints, padded sun visors.

Inner fenders for added protection.

Buick   The solid feeling for '73.

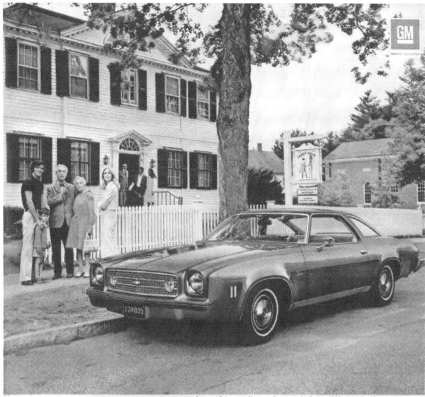

Laguna Colonnade Hardtop Coupe at the Rockwell Museum, Stockbridge, Mass.

Introducing Laguna. The new top-of-the-line Chevelle.

Good news, Chevelle people. You can move up to more car without leaving the make you love most.

Laguna is a new kind of Chevelle, the top of the line.

The distinctively styled front end is covered completely by resilient, protective urethane to resist dents.

Laguna has among other things a special body-color rear bumper.

Inside: special fabrics, special steering wheel and woodgrain accents.

Laguna, like all '73 Chevelles, has new front disc brakes, flow-through power ventilation, more glass area for improved visibility and more back seat leg room.

There's a power-operated moonroof you can add.

You're going to like the Laguna. A lot.

1973 Chevrolet. Building a better way to see the U.S.A. Chevrolet

Introducing Laguna. The new top-of-the-line Chevelle.

Good news, Chevelle people. You can move up to more car without leaving the make you love most.

Laguna is a new kind of Chevelle, the top of the line.

The distinctively styled front end is covered completely by resilient, protective urethane to resist dents.

Laguna has among other things a special body-color rear bumper.

Inside: special fabrics, special steering wheel and woodgrain accents.

Laguna, like all '73 Chevelles, has new front disc brakes, flow-through power ventilation, more glass area for improved visibility and more back seat leg room.

There's a power-operated moonroof you can add.

You're going to like the Laguna. A lot.

1973 Chevrolet. Building a better way to see the U.S.A.

Paris Accords End Vietnam War 27th January 1973

We had long ago grown tired and fed-up with the ongoing Vietnam War (known in Vietnam as the American War). US troops in Vietnam had dropped from a peak of 536,100 in 1968, to just 24,200 by the start of 1973,[1] as President Nixon continued to pull out the troops. Nixon and his advisors believed there could never be a military victory for the USA in Vietnam, seeking instead an "honorable" settlement– one which prepared South Vietnam to fight the Viet Cong alone.

Above: Signing of the Paris Peace Accords, 27th Jan 1973.
Right: The signed *Agreement on Ending the War and Restoring Peace in Viet Nam.*

In January 1973, representatives from the USA, South Vietnam, North Vietnam, and the Viet Cong, met in Paris to thrash out an agreement to end the war and restore peace in Vietnam. The Paris Peace Accords were signed on 27th January.

The Accords included an immediate ceasefire, the removal of all US troops, the return of all prisoners of war (POWs), and the dismantling of all US bases, bringing an end to America's 8-year direct involvement in the war. The government of South Vietnam would remain in power, and a demilitarized zone around the 17th parallel would remain in effect until the two Vietnams could be reunited peacefully.

Not surprisingly, the cease-fire did not last long.

[1] americanwarlibrary.com/vietnam/vwatl.htm.

Operation Homecoming

With the Paris Accords signed, the release of POWs could begin. Known as Operation Homecoming, the first of 591 American POWs boarded flights back to the USA on 12th Feb.

American POWs being escorted to their flights out of Hanoi.

Department of Defense photo captioned: *The returnees maintained their composure until it was clear that they were again safe under American control. No one was silent as this Air Force C-141 Starlifter left the runway at Hanoi. The photographer, TSgt Robert N. Denham, USAF, observed that "You could hear the shouts and cheers all over the aircraft" on this 28 March 1973 flight.*

The released POWs were received at one of three designated receiving locations within Vietnam. They were then flown to Clark Air Force Base in the Philippines for physical and mental evaluations, medical treatment and debriefings. The final leg of their journey brought them to Kelly Field Air Force Base in San Antonio, Texas.

TWA figures if you like our 747 you'll love our 1011.

First Class.
Our 747 First Class is big and gracious, our 1011 First Class is big and gracious. Plus we made part of it a dining room with big, comfortable swivel seats so you can dine with friends. You can even make reservations as you would in a restaurant.

Coach.
You like Coach to be roomy? You'll love how roomy this Coach is. And so you won't feel crowded, we put in unique two-by-two seating. You'll never be more than one seat from the aisle.

Technology.
TWA's 1011 is even more advanced than the 747. It's the most advanced plane ever built. In fact, it uses some of the same technology that landed our men on the moon. Treat yourself to a trip on TWA's 1011. It's everything an airplane should be.

TWA is what travel should be.

TWA figures if you like our 747 you'll love our 1011.

First Class. Our 747 First Class is big and gracious, our 1011 First Class is big and gracious. Plus we made part of it a dining room with big, comfortable swivel seats so you can dine with friends. You can even make reservations as you would in a restaurant.

Coach. You like Coach to be roomy? You'll love how roomy this Coach is. And so you won't feel crowded, we put in unique two-by-two seating. You'll never be more than one seat from the aisle.

Technology. TWA's 1011 is even more advanced than the 747. It's the most advanced plane ever built. In fact, it uses some of the same technology that landed our men on the moon. Treat yourself to a trip on TWA's 1011. It's everything an airplane should be.

TWA is what travel should be.

On 17th May, live daily television broadcasts of the Watergate hearings began. Outraged viewers watched as the Senate Select Committee on Presidential Campaign Activities uncovered widespread evidence of bribery, political espionage, evidence tampering and illegal wire-tapping of thousands of citizens. It was the scandal that would bring down a president and forever scar American politics.

Members of President Nixon's re-election committee had broken into the Democratic National Committee's headquarters in the Watergate building one year earlier. They stole documents and bugged the telephones. On their return visit, they were caught by a vigilant guard.

Nixon Knew of Cover-Up Plan

Nixon Tells Editors, 'I'm Not a Crook'

Watergate Panel Aims at Deeper Campaign Probe

3 Top Nixon Aides Tied to Cover-Up

President Taped Talks, Phone Calls; Lawyer Ties Ehrlichman to Payments

Watergate newspaper headlines from 1973.

Movies about Watergate, *All the Presidents Men* (Warner Bros. 1976) and *The Post* (20th Century Fox, 2017).

The President vehemently denied having links to the "burglars", while secretly paying hush money to cover-up the crimes, and instructing the CIA to obstruct an FBI investigation. The public believed his lies, giving him a landslide re-election victory.

Washington Post reporters Bob Woodward and Carl Bernstein received damning proof of illegal espionage from a whistle-blower known as *Deep Throat*. As Nixon's aides began to turn against him, the House Judiciary Committee voted to impeach the President for obstruction of justice, abuse of power, and contempt of Congress. Nixon resigned in August 1974. His crimes were pardoned by his successor, President Gerald Ford.

Nuclear Bomb Testing

Remember when dropping nuclear bombs was commonplace? For more than 40 years, the Nuclear Arms Race gave the USA and USSR the pretext needed to test nuclear bombs on a massive scale. Nearly 1,700 bombs were dropped by the superpowers, most of them during the '60s and '70s. A further 300 were tested by China, France, and the UK. These tests served to understand the effectiveness and capacity of each bomb type. They also acted as a deterrent to enemy nations.

In 1973, the US carried out 24 nuclear tests, mostly at the Nevada Proving Grounds, while USSR tested 17 nuclear bombs.

On 9th May, New Zealand and Australian governments took France to the International Court of Justice in an attempt to ban atmospheric nuclear tests in the South Pacific region. France switched to underground testing the following year.

Underwater nuclear test at Bikini Atoll. In 1963 the two superpowers signed a Nuclear Test Ban treaty, limiting tests to underground only. Space, atmospheric, and underwater tests ceased.

US troops and observers witness the detonation of *Small Boy* at the Nevada Proving Grounds in 1962, (prior to the Test Ban).

Although most of the test sites were largely uninhabited by humans, some of them were densely populated. The effects of radioactive fallout plagued local populations for years afterward.

Yom Kippur War 6th – 25th October 1973

Egyptian forces crossing the Suez Canal into the Sinai Peninsula.

On 6th October, the Jewish holiday of Yom Kippur, a coalition of Arab states led by Egypt and Syria launched a surprise attack against Israel. Egyptian troops swept into Sinai Peninsula, while Syrian troops attacked Israeli forces in the Golan Heights. Both nations aimed to take back regions they had lost to Israeli during the six-day war of 1967.

Caught off-guard, the Israelis were initially forced to retreat, retaking lost ground a few days later once troop reinforcements arrived.

With the Soviets supporting the Arab coalition, the US felt compelled to aid Israel by sending a full-scale air-lift of military equipment. The Arab members of OPEC responded to this by implementing an oil embargo against all the countries supporting Israel.

Amidst threats of direct action by the Soviets and much shuttling between nations by the US Secretary of State Henry Kissinger, a UN-brokered ceasefire was ultimately reached. The years-long stalemate in peace negotiations had been broken. Further talks would lead to the 1979 Egypt–Israel peace treaty and Israel's withdrawal from the Sinai Peninsula.

Israeli troops retake the Sinai Peninsula, Oct 1973.

OPEC Oil Embargo and Oil Crisis   19th October 1973

The oil embargo imposed by Arab members of the Organization of Petroleum Exporting Countries (OPEC) during the Yom Kippur War directly targeted the USA, the UK, Canada, Japan, and other western countries considered allies of Israel, who relied on oil supplies from the Middle East. Shipments to these nations were immediately suspended.

The lack of alternative providers caused an immediate jump in the price of oil. Prices continued rising, from $2.90 a barrel before the embargo to $11.65 a barrel in January 1974. The impact of this fourfold increase on the global economy was significant and severe.

In response to the embargo, the US government imposed fuel rationing and lowered speed limits to reduce consumption.

Gas stations ran out of fuel as motorists queued to fill up. Prices could rise several times a day, causing motorists to panic-buy.

In the US, soaring oil prices and a falling US dollar strained businesses, with many closing or laying off workers. Unemployment rose sharply, GDP plummeted to negative figures (-0.50% in 1974) and lack of liquidity triggered a massive stock market crash.

A similar scenario played out across much of the Western world, and the period 1973-1975 would be plagued by economic recession.

The oil embargo was eventually lifted in March 1974. However, the devastating effects would linger for most of the '70s. The oil crisis had highlighted the importance of energy security and the need for alternative energy sources and conservation measures.

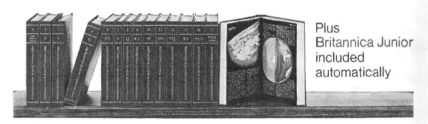

Smith-Corona: the graduation gift to help make sure there's another graduation.

Congratulations. It's not every day your son or daughter gets accepted by a college.

The work, of course, is going to get a lot tougher. Which is why a Smith-Corona makes an ideal graduation gift. It can help with saving time, spelling, and most important, with organization.

Add to that the right amount of application and ability and you can begin looking forward to next graduation.

But why Smith-Corona?
Because all typewriters are not the same.

If you compare durability and features, plus our years of experience in making portables (especially electrics), you'll know why more people in the world buy Smith-Corona Electric Portables than any other.

And why you should, too.

We think we make better students.
We know we make better typewriters.

Troubles in Northern Ireland

The 30-year-long nationalist campaign in Northern Ireland, known as *The Troubles*, peaked in 1972 with almost 500 people killed in battles. The bloodshed continued during the first half of 1973, as Roman Catholic Republicans (IRA) fought against Protestant Ulster Unionists and the British military. Although often mistaken for a war of religion, *The Troubles* was in fact a political war. The Republicans were fighting for the reunification of Northern Ireland with the Republic of Ireland. The Unionists sought to keep Northern Ireland as part of the UK.

British Troops arrest a suspected Republican on the first day of *Internment* (imprisonment without trial), 9th Aug 1971.

An injured woman is comforted by a British soldier in the aftermath of an IRA bomb blast in Donegall Street, Belfast. 20th March 1972.

The Troubles flared up in the late '60s with British troops arriving to quell the violence. The troops remained, patrolling Northern Ireland's streets for 37 years. Although their role was officially to be neutral peace-keepers, they were permitted to imprison IRA suspects without trial, and were condemned for covertly supporting the Unionists.

Peace Walls were hastily erected throughout the cities and suburbs of Northern Ireland, physically separating Republicans from Unionist neighborhoods.

A total of 34 km (21 miles) of Peace Walls were built by the British Government, which in recent years have become something of a tourist attraction.

8th Mar– A referendum was held to determine whether Northern Ireland should remain part of the United Kingdom or join the Republic of Ireland. Republicans boycotted the poll. With only Unionists voting, the result was a near unanimous 98.9% vote to remain in the UK.

Violent attacks, waged by both sides, occurred on polling day. Several bombs went off across Northern Ireland, while the Provisional IRA (PIRA–militant faction of the IRA) used the date to begin its Mainland Campaign by attacking military targets, government buildings and infrastructure outside of Northern Ireland.

Above: Street scene in central London after an IRA bomb exploded, 8th Mar 1973.

Below: *Bloody Sunday*, 30th Jan 1972. The British Army faced off against protesters in Derry, Northern Ireland.

8th Mar– The PIRA exploded two car bombs in London, injuring over 200 people. Two additional car bombs were diffused. London had not seen such devastation since WWII.

28th Jun– The Northern Ireland Assembly was created with the aim of establishing a power-sharing governmental body.

9th Dec– The Sunningdale Agreement was signed between the mainstream Nationalist and Unionist parties, the British and the Irish governments. The Agreement was an attempt produce a political solution to Northern Ireland, but was opposed by the IRA and many Unionists, leaving it largely unworkable. Within four months, the Agreement was dismantled.

3-Day Work Week for the UK

Soaring inflation and a cap on public sector pay rises left many British workers struggling from a drop in real wages. In October 1973, the powerful National Union of Mineworkers (NUM) demanded a fair deal for its members–a 35% pay increase to bring salaries on par with other industries. The ruling Conservative Party soundly rejected the request.

NUM members voted against strike action, choosing a ban on overtime instead. The ban halved electricity supply overnight, as coal stockpiles had been largely depleted during a six-week miner's strike in 1972. Electricity supply struggled to keep up with the winter demand.

On 13th Dec, in a bid to lower usage, Prime Minister Edward Heath announced a three-day work week commencing 31st Dec. Electricity would be rationed to homes on a rotational basis. Millions were laid-off as business struggled to remain operational.

Employees working by candlelight, Jan 1974.

Five weeks later, NUM members voted in favor of a full strike, having rejected the National Coal Board's 16% pay rise offer.

Assuming public support for tough government over trade union demands, Heath called a snap general election. He did not win re-election.

The miner's strike and the three-day work week lasted until Mar '74. Its end was brought about by the return of Harold Wilson (prime minister 1964-'70 and 1974-'76), and his agreement to the full 35% wage increase.

A 3-DAY WEEK BRITAIN

MILLIONS of workers will go on to a three or four-day week from Monday unless the miners' leaders decide today to order a ballot on the Coal Board's pay offer.

Rotas are being drawn up by the Electricity Boards and firms will be forbidden to use electricity for two days a week.

Keeping up your spirits!

By HARVEY ELLIOTT

BRITONS are deter-

For people who can't leave well enough alone, look what you can do with a Banquet Turkey Cookin' Bag entree.

Giblet gravy and sliced turkey. Nobody makes it faster or better than Banquet, but if you want to make it fancier, here's how:

Take one Banquet Giblet Gravy and Sliced Turkey Cookin' Bag entree from your freezer and prepare. Top with turkey, then add gravy. Garnish with parsley, pimiento and a sprinkling of curry powder. Serve with snow peas and kumquats, accompanied by an avocado and cherry tomato salad.

Banquet. When you start with great food you end with a great meal.

GENERAL ELECTRIC INVENTS FLASHBAR™ 10.

The revolutionary flash that lets you take 10 pictures without replacing the flash.

The FlashBar 10 array was invented by General Electric for the new Polaroid® SX-70 Land Camera.

FlashBar 10 is the new flash system that lets you take ten pictures without replacing the flash. Now there are as many flashes as pictures in a film pack.

FlashBar 10 is compact. So small you can hide it in your hand.

FlashBar 10 is fast. Ten rapid-fire pictures in less than thirty seconds. Flash five. Flip the GE FlashBar array. Flash five more.

FlashBar 10 is powerful. You can take flash shots up to twenty feet away. Its new high-output lamps give you almost twice the light of standard flashcubes.

FlashBar 10 is reliable. It lessens your chance of wasting a picture by flashing the same flash twice. The camera scans the FlashBar 10 array electronically and picks the next flash on that side to be fired.

FlashBar 10 gives color-true pictures. It's covered by a color-corrected shield that's made to match the Polaroid SX-70 film.

The FlashBar 10 array is now available at stores in your area.

FlashBar 10. Another flash of genius from General Electric.

Flash five. Flip the FlashBar 10 array. Flash five more.

FlashBar is the General Electric trademark for its flash array. Polaroid® by Polaroid Corp.

GENERAL ⊛ ELECTRIC

General Electric Invents FlashBar 10.

The revolutionary flash that lets you take 10 pictures without replacing the flash.

The FlashBar 10 array was invented by General Electric for the new Polaroid SX-70 Land Camera.

FlashBar 10 is the new flash system that lets you take ten pictures without replacing the flash. Now there are as many flashes as pictures in a film pack.

FlashBar 10 is compact. So small you can hide it in your hand.

FlashBar 10 is fast. Ten rapid-fire pictures in less than thirty seconds. Flash five. Flip the GE FlashBar array. Flash five more.

FlashBar 10 is powerful. You can take flash shots up to twenty feet away. Its new high-output lamps give you almost twice the light of standard flashcubes.

FlashBar 10 is reliable. It lessens your chance of wasting a picture by flashing the same flash twice. The camera scans the FlashBar 10 array electronically and picks the next flash on that side to be fired.

FlashBar 10 gives color-true pictures. It's covered by a color-corrected shield that's made to match the Polaroid SX-70 film.

The FlashBar 10 array is now available at stores in your area.

FlashBar 10. Another flash of genius from General Electric.

Flash five. Flip the FlashBar 10. Flash five more.

Roe v. Wade 22nd January 1973

The US Supreme Court's landmark ruling for Roe v. Wade held (7 to 2) that a set of Texas laws criminalizing abortion in most instances was unduly restrictive and violated a woman's constitutional right of privacy. With this ruling, women across America had a constitutional right to choose to have an abortion.

The case had been brought by the plaintiff, Norma McCorvey, (aka Jane Roe) against the district attorney of Dallas county, Texas, Henry Wade. The ruling gave women the right to make their own reproductive and health decisions. It was a major victory for women's rights.

Right: Norma McCorvey in 1979.
Below: A pro-choice street march.

The decision split the nation into pro-life anti-abortionists, who believe life begins at conception and the fetus must be protected by God and by state law, and pro-choice believers who argue that the fetus is not a whole person and the right to decide belongs to the mother. Activists on both sides kept the controversy intense and sometimes violent.

On 24th June 2022, the US Supreme Court overturned Roe v. Wade, removing 50 years of legal protection for women requiring an abortion.

Operation Wounded Knee

On 27th February, around 200 members of the Oglala Lakota (Sioux) tribe arrived in the small town of Wounded Knee in South Dakota and were quickly encircled by police roadblocks. They came to discuss the corrupt dealings of their tribal president and to demand his removal. They found themselves "occupying" the town.

Their protests grew to cover a range of grievances, including the unjust and oppressive treatment of Native Americans by the government, the policies of forced assimilation, forced relocations, and the erasure of their culture. In addition, they highlighted the government's failure to honor signed treaties, such as their right to their traditional lands.

The occupation lasted 71 days, with three people killed in shootouts with Federal Marshals. It brought national attention and a renewed push for Native American rights and self-determination.

At the 1973 Oscar ceremony, Marlon Brando refused his *Best Actor* award in protest against the bad treatment of Native Americans by the film industry and the government's actions at Wounded Knee. He sent native American activist and actor Sacheen Littlefeather in his place to read his statement. Littlefeather was booed by the audience, and her career was ruined as Hollywood blacklisted her.

In 2022, at the age of 75, Littlefeather received an apology from the Academy of Motion Picture Arts and Sciences.

Endangered Species Act

The Endangered Species Act (ESA), signed into law by President Nixon on 28th December, was seen as a huge win for the conservation movement at a time when ecological issues were not given much consideration. The ESA aimed to protect threatened or endangered animals, plants, and ecosystems, establishing a framework for their conservation and recovery.

Nixon signs into law the Endangered Species Act, 28th Dec 1973.

Human encroachment and destruction of flora and fauna habitats, pollution, hunting, and collecting had caused an exponential rise in species extinctions and potential extinctions throughout the 20th Century.

Under the ESA, US federal agencies would be required to implement plans to aid in the conservation and recovery of any species listed as threatened or endangered, including their habitats.

The American bald eagle, the peregrine falcon, and the gray wolf are some of the animals, together with more than 1,600 species listed, which have been saved thanks to actions under the ESA.

PEPPERONI AND SONY.

A screen almost the size of a kid's baseball glove. 7 diagonal inches.

A playing time of over 4 hours without recharging. That's a ballgame _and_ a Western.

A neat 15-lb. set. With space for the optional batteries right inside.

Sony built it especially for outdoor pleasures like hot dogs or pepperoni.

No baloney.

Pepperoni and Sony.

A screen almost the size of a kid's baseball glove. 7 diagonal inches.

A playing time of over 4 hours without recharging. That's a ballgame and a Western.

A neat 15-lb set. With space for the optional batteries right inside.

Sony built it especially for outdoor pleasures like hot dogs or pepperoni.

No baloney.

Tuning in to Television

The television was our must-have appliance of the mid-20th century, taking pride of place in our family or living rooms. By 1973, nearly every US household owned a television,[1] with more than half of them being color sets. Although color TVs had been around since the early '50s, and color broadcasts had become commonplace since the mid-'60s, the switch from black and white to color in homes was very slow.

Outside the USA, some countries like Canada and the UK were catching up with color TV ownership and broadcasting. Australia, however, would wait till 1975 for its first color television broadcasts.

Elsewhere in the world, rates of television ownership lagged even further behind.

In many countries, television networks were government owned or subsidized, allowing for more focus on serious documentaries and news, without the constant concern of generating advertising revenue.

Carroll O'Connor and Mike Evans in *All in the Family* (CBS. 1971-1979).

Most Popular TV Shows of 1973 [3]

1	All in the Family	11	Adam-12
2	Sanford and Son	12	The Flip Wilson Show
3	Hawaii Five-O	13	Marcus Welby, M.D.
4	Maude	14	Cannon
5	Bridget Loves Bernie	15	Here's Lucy
=	The NBC Sunday Mystery Movie	16	The Bob Newhart Show
7	The Mary Tyler Moore Show	17	Tuesday Movie of the Week
=	Gunsmoke	18	Monday Night Football
9	The Wonderful World of Disney	19	The Partridge Family
10	Ironside	=	The Waltons
		=	Medical Center

[1] americancentury.omeka.wlu.edu/items/show/136.
[2] tvobscurities.com/articles/color60s/.
[3] Nielsen Media Research 1973-'74 season of top-rated primetime television series in the USA.

The Mary Tyler Moore Show portrayed Moore's character as a financially independent working woman, which was still a rarity at the time. The show would win 29 Emmy Awards during its eight-year run, and launch three spin-offs: *Rhoda*, *Phyllis*, and *Lou Grant*.

Valerie Harper, Edward Asner, Cloris Leachman, Gavin MacLeod, Mary Tyler Moore, and Ted Knight in *The Mary Tyler Moore Show* (CBS. 1970–1977).

Although sitcoms and variety programs remained popular in 1973, a new wave of intense TV dramas was keeping us glued to our television sets. A slew of police, detective, or medical themed primetime TV programs hit our screens in the late '60s, and we were hooked.

Six of the twenty top-ranking TV series for 1973 were medical or crime themed programs, most lasting well into the decade.

Airing for an impressive 12 seasons, *Hawaii Five-O* was largely shot on location in Honolulu. It followed a special police task force fighting organized crime across the Hawaiian Islands.

Zulu, Jack Lord, James MacArthur and Kam Fong in *Hawaii Five-O* (CBS. 1968-1980).

The original series ended in 1980, making it the longest running TV crime show at that time. A 2010 remake ran for ten seasons.

David Hasselhoff and Trish Stewart in *The Young and the Restless* (Bell Dramatic Serial & Corday 1973-present, Colombia 1974-2001, Sony 2002-present).

Telly Savalas in *Kojak* (Universal Television, 1973-'78).

The television networks were quick to turn out new programs to keep us tuning in. Here are a few of the new programs that aired for the first time in 1973: *Kojak, The Six Million Dollar Man, Barnaby Jones, The Midnight Special, The Tomorrow Show, Police Story, Some Mothers Do 'Ave 'Em* (BBC1), and *The Young and the Restless* (1973-present).

Scott Brady in
Police Story (NBC. 1973-'77).

Lee Majors in *The Six Million Dollar Man* (ABC. 1973-'78).

Choosing a color TV is no spur-of-the-moment decision. You need some pretty strong reasons to pick one set over another.

Like the Quatrecolor *modular chassis* that makes servicing quick and easy. Because 75% of all our circuitry is built onto 5 circuit boards.

In fact, the National Electronics Association rated the Quatrecolor CT-701 as the easiest to service of all color televisions they tested in plant through June 1973.

Of course, we want those service calls to be few and far between. So we engineer every Quatrecolor set with *100% solid-state* circuitry. To run cooler and last longer. Because the only tube is the picture tube.

And what a picture tube. We call it *Pana-Matrix*. It surrounds each color dot with a black background. So you get bright, vivid colors. And a sharp picture.

And you don't have to worry about drops or surges in voltage ruining the picture. Because Quatrecolor has a special automatic voltage regulator circuit with SCR (Silicon Control Rectifier) that maintains the correct voltage level.

You won't have to fiddle with a bunch of knobs to keep the picture beautiful, either. Because Panasonic gives you O-Lock. One button that electronically controls color, tint, contrast and brightness.

And O-Lock's active color and tint circuits automatically seek out and maintain the best color picture. Even when you change channels, or atmospheric conditions affect the signal.

Quatrecolor. From 17" portables up to 25" consoles (measured diagonally).

After all we put into them, you owe it to yourself to go see the picture that comes out of them.

Panasonic. Just slightly ahead of our time.

1973 in Cinema and Film

As cinema-going viewers, our interests and focus had turned away from traditional classic Hollywood mainstays, bounding with optimism and happy endings. We were seeking more depth, more pain and reality.

Highest Paid Stars

1. Clint Eastwood
2. Ryan O'Neal
3. Steve McQueen
4. Burt Reynolds
5. Robert Redford
6. Barbra Streisand
7. Paul Newman
8. Charles Bronson
9. John Wayne
10. Marlon Brando

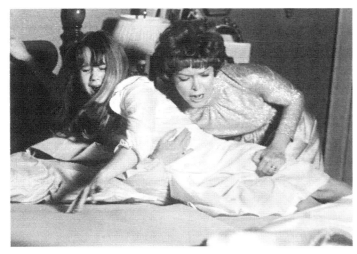

Linda Blair and Ellen Burstyn starred in the controversial and shocking 1973 horror blockbuster *The Exorcist*. Audiences flocked to the cinema, despite its many grotesquely disturbing and violent scenes.

By 1973, a new breed of directors like Francis Ford Coppola, Martin Scorsese, George Lucas, and Stanly Kubrik demanded more artistic control. They bravely tackled darker, more gritty, pessimistic themes of war, crime, depression and inner turmoil. The era of big cinema houses owning their actors and controlling their directors had ended.

1973 film debuts

Laura Dern	White Lightning
Stan Lee	The Year 01
Emilio Estevez	Badlands
Tatum O'Neal	Paper Moon
Kathleen Quinlan	American Graffiti
Stellan Skarsgård	Anita—ur en tonärsflickas dagbok

* From en.wikipedia.org/wiki/1973_in_film.

Comic-book writer, editor, and publisher Stan Lee spent 44 years doing voice overs and making cameo appearances for Marvel film and TV projects. Lee co-created many iconic superheroes including the X-Men, Spider Man, The Hulk, Iron Man, Thor, Doctor Strange, Ant-Man, The Wasp, Black Panther and Scarlet Witch.

Top Grossing Films of the Year

1	The Exorcist	Warner Bros. Pictures	$88,500,000
2	The Sting	Universal Pictures	$79,000,000
3	American Graffiti	Universal Pictures	$55,900,000
4	Papillon	Allied Artists	$22,500,000
5	The Way We Were	Columbia Pictures	$22,457,000
6	Magnum Force	Warner Bros. Pictures	$20,100,000
7	Last Tango in Paris	United Artists	$16,711,000
8	Paper Moon	Paramount Pictures	$16,559,000
9	Live and Let Die	United Artists	$15,925,000
10	The Devil in Miss Jones	VCX Ltd./MB Productions	$15,000,000

* From en.wikipedia.org/wiki/1973_in_film by box office gross in the USA.

George Lucas' nostalgic coming of age movie *American Graffiti* starred little known actors Harrison Ford and Richard Dreyfuss. The film's use of pop songs throughout has since become a staple for films targeting younger audiences.

Based on the 1969 autobiography of French convict Henri Charrière, *Papillon* follows the horrors of life in a French Guyana prison camp. The decades that pass, and the many escape attempts by inmates Charrière "Papillon" (Steve McQueen) and Louis Dega (Dustin Hoffman) are chronicled in this grueling grim historical epic.

A Decade of Disasters

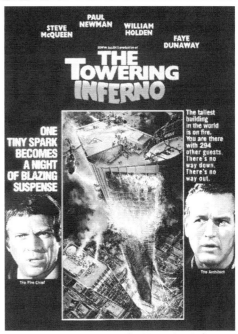

The Poseidon Adventure
(20th Century Fox, 1972).

The Towering Inferno
(20th Century Fox, 1974).

The decade of the '70s saw the disaster movie genre reign supreme at the box office. Large casts, multiple plot lines, life or death calamities and impossible tales of survival kept us on the edge of our seats.

Earthquake (Universal, 1974).

Tidalwave (Toho, 1973).

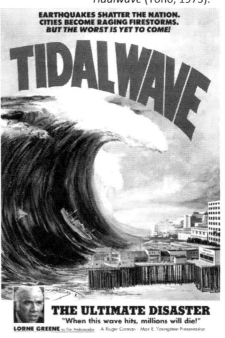

Rocky Horror Show Debuts

Dr. Frank-N-Furter portrayed in the German stage show of 2005.

Reminiscent of B-grade mid-century sci-fi horror films, *The Rocky Horror Show* mixed '70s Glam Rock music with outrageously gaudy costumes worn by sexually questionable other-worldly characters.

With music and lyrics by Richard O'Brien, the show opened at the tiny experimental Royal Court Theatre in London on 19th June. It ran for 2,960 performances, closing in 1980 after 17 months on the West End. It has since been staged across Europe, Asia, the Americas and Australia.

Set in the eerie gothic castle of eccentric transvestite scientist Dr. Frank-N-Furter, the crazy plot follows the visit of Brad and Janet (two lost travelers) during a night storm.

With catchy songs and effervescent dance sequences, the fantasy musical provided a frivolous escape from our real-world drama. Its disregard for sexual norms was ground-breaking for musicals.

The Rocky Horror Show opened in the USA in March 1974 at Los Angele's Roxy Theatre. 20th Century Fox immediately secured the film rights.

The 1975 film, *The Rocky Horror Picture Show,* quickly became an international cult classic. Midnight screenings continue worldwide, with audience members dressing in drag to interact with the film.

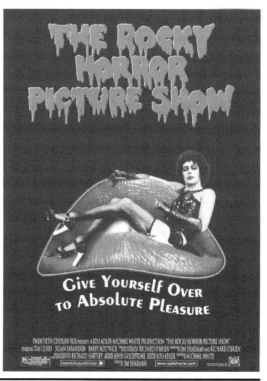

Magnavox 4-channel sound. It fills your room without emptying your wallet.

It doesn't take a lot to fill a room. Just a Magnavox 4-channel system. For just a little.

Whichever way you want your 4-channel sound—matrix records, FM broadcasts, enhanced stereo from your present records—we've got you surrounded. With music of startlingly realistic depth and separation. From components that are prematched by audio experts, not by chance;

A 3-speed automatic turn-table with magnetic cartridge, diamond stylus and acrylic dustcover;

Four 2-way air-suspension speakers sealed in walnut-finished enclosures;

And an AM/FM stereo receiver that's sensitive enough to make your hi-fi-nut nephew envious, powerful enough to make your next-door neighbor furious.

The complete system is loaded with everything else you'd expect. But at a price you'd never expect.

Ask your Magnavox dealer about Model 1817, the compact 1816, and other Magnavox 4-channel sound systems. You'll be surprised how little big sounds costs.

Magnavox. You heard right.

The Greatest Year in Rock History

The early '70s saw musicians turn away from the chart-topping feel-good melodies of previous years. Singer-songwriters like Elton John, Cat Stevens, James Taylor, Marvin Gaye, and Carly Simon looked inwards, exploring their emotions and anxieties, while Alice Cooper, Pink Floyd, and others, reached out to the aimless and confused.

This set the stage for the year 1973, arguably the greatest year in rock history, thanks to the release of multiple seminal rock albums. On both sides of the pond, American and British rock bands put out timeless classics, which still influence the music we listen to today.

Pink Floyd's *The Dark Side of the Moon* explored themes of conflict, death, and mental health. The album became one of the most influential and best-selling albums of all time.

Greetings from Asbury Park, N.J.–the debut album for Bruce Springsteen–established the artist as a noteworthy songwriter, tackling the difficult social issues of teenagers and young adults.

At the same time, Aerosmith's released their debut album titled *Aerosmith*. However, the album did not perform well for the band. Production and promotional effort was lacking, and band members lacked confidence in their musical abilities. In particular, lead vocalist Steven Tyler failed to showcase his trademark screams that he later became renowned for.

Elton John's double LP *Goodbye Yellow Brick Road* was released late in 1973. The album raced to the top of the charts, becoming the best-selling album in the US for 1974. It sold more than 20 million copies worldwide, and is widely considered his life's masterpiece.

Billion Dollar Babies became the most successful album for the 5-piece band Alice Cooper. Two years later the band's lead vocalist would adopt the name as his stage name, drawing inspiration from horror films and vaudeville to establish himself as the father of "Shock Rock".

The year's long list of notable rock albums included: Queen's debut album *Queen,* Led Zeppelin's *Houses Of The Holy,* The Who's *Quadrophenia,* Black Sabbath's *Sabbath Bloody Sabbath, and* Deep Purple's *Who Do We Think We Are!*

15th June– Marvin Gaye's single *Let's Get It On* was released, becoming the Billboard R&B Song of the Year.

6th Aug– Stevie Wonder spent four days in a coma after a car crash in North Carolina. He had won a Grammy for *Best Male Pop Vocal Performance* earlier in the year.

1973 Billboard Top 30 Songs

	Artist	Song Title
1	Tony Orlando and Dawn	Tie a Yellow Ribbon Round the Ole Oak Tree
2	Jim Croce	Bad, Bad Leroy Brown
3	Roberta Flack	Killing Me Softly with His Song
4	Marvin Gaye	Let's Get It On
5	Paul McCartney & Wings	My Love
6	Kris Kristofferson	Why Me
7	Elton John	Crocodile Rock
8	Billy Preston	Will It Go Round in Circles
9	Carly Simon	You're So Vain
10	Diana Ross	Touch Me in the Morning

Roberta Flack, 1976.

Kris Kristofferson, 1978.

Diana Ross, 22ⁿᵈ Aug 1976.

Cher, 22ⁿᵈ Dec 1972.

Artist	Song Title
11 Vicki Lawrence	The Night the Lights Went Out in Georgia
12 Clint Holmes	Playground in My Mind
13 Stories	Brother Louie
14 Helen Reddy	Delta Dawn
15 Billy Paul	Me and Mrs. Jones
16 The Edgar Winter Group	Frankenstein
17 Dobie Gray	Drift Away
18 Sweet	Little Willy
19 Stevie Wonder	You Are the Sunshine of My Life
20 Cher	Half-Breed

Elton John on the *Cher Show*, 1975.

Carly Simon, 1978.

21 The Isley Brothers	That Lady
22 Sylvia Robinson	Pillow Talk
23 Grand Funk Railroad	We're an American Band
24 Dr. John	Right Place Wrong Time
25 Skylark	Wildflower
26 Stevie Wonder	Superstition
27 Paul Simon	Loves Me Like a Rock
28 Maureen McGovern	The Morning After
29 John Denver	Rocky Mountain High
30 Stealers Wheel	Stuck in the Middle with You

* From the *Billboard* top 30 singles of 1973.

If we added any more, we'd have to give lessons on how to use it.

Public Service Band. For continuous weather, fire and police calls.
Dial Light Switch. For tuning in the dark.
FM Band. For your favorite rock or classical music.
Continuous Tone Control. Adjusts the treble-base balance.
Separate Volume Control. No resetting the volume each time you turn the radio on.
AM Band. If you get tired of FM and Public Service Band.
Unusual Tuning Dial. The numbers move instead of the pointer.
Big 4" Speaker. For big, beautiful sound.
Special Indicator Meter. Shows station strength. Or battery strength.
Automatic Frequency Control. Stops station drift on FM and Public Service Band.
Continuous Squelch Control. Filters out interstation and intersignal noise.
Batteries. It comes with 4 Panasonic "C" batteries. It also works on house current.

The RF-1060 Portable Radio
Panasonic. Just slightly ahead of our time.

There used to be a drawback to playing tapes in your car. A bumpy ride could distort the music. That's why we gave our latest car stereo, the CQ-959, something called Vertical Head Movement. It works like shock absorbers.

With Vertical Head Movement, the tape head doesn't bounce. Even when your car does. That way, there's no distortion in your music. Which leaves you free to get the full enjoyment from our other features.

Like our 12-watt dual-channel amplifier, which gives clear, sharp stereo sound.
And our tone, volume and balance controls. So if you want more guitar and less bass, or vice versa, you can get it.

There's even a distant/local switch. So you can listen to an FM station that's nearby or one that's farther away. And get stable reception from either.

The new CQ-959 from Panasonic. The music is smooth, even when the ride isn't.

Our new car stereo has FM, AM, FM stereo, 8-track, and shock absorbers.

Fashion Trends of the 1970s

By the early '70s in the world of fashion, we had clearly lost our way and were looking for answers. This was a decade without guidance and without rules. Trends caught on and shifted quickly. Fashions were varied and experimental. Pants got wider, skirts got shorter, and boots got taller. And within a season the trends reversed. Anything was possible, everything was acceptable.

Walking down any street you would have found skirts worn mini, midi, or full length. Pants could be slim-fit, wide, or bell bottomed, hip-hugging or waist-clinching. Tops might be tie-dye swirl-patterned or bold solids. Shirts came long and loose, or tight and tailored.

Daywear pants-suit and skirt-suit.

Dresses came in all shapes and lengths too. They could be short Mod shifts, or calico lace prairie-style. They could be tailored with shirt-style collars and buttoned-down fronts. They could be long and loose caftans, flowing maxi-dresses, or waisted tailored-cut with belts and A-line skirts taken straight from the '50s.

Patchwork maxi-dresses by Yves Saint Laurent.

The hippie and psychedelic fashions of the late '60s were adopted and modified by mainstream non-hippies into more elegant structured forms. Caftans, prairie dresses, patchwork fabrics, shawls, tassels and beads hit the runways, and the streets, in the early '70s.

Elizabeth Taylor during her bohemian period, 1969.

Maudie James models Thea Porter patchwork dress, 1970.

Weipert and Burda fashion show, 1972.

In contrast to the hippie trends, Mod dresses of the early '60s made a comeback. Space-age synthetics and plastics, widely used in the '60s, were replaced with comfortable cottons and stretch knits. In winter, tunic dresses could be worn over turtlenecks, with woolen stockings or thigh-high boots.

Mod mini dresses worn with white boots or shoes, early 1970s.

The '70s were the first full decade where pants for women gained mainstream acceptance, and we couldn't get enough of them. Pants could be worn for any occasion—pants-suits for the office, silky patterns for evenings, or blocks and geometrics dressed down for daywear. And let's not forget blue jeans, the staple of casual wear for both men and women.

Day wear pants from the Sears Spring/ Summer catalog, 1970.

In the early '70s men and women wore their pants gently flared at the base. As the decade progressed, the flares got wider and wider, exploding into bell-bottoms by the mid-'70s.

Embroidered denim.

Flared knit polyester pants.

Flared silky jumpsuits.

Get it on.

Move out with Pedwin. Padded tops and lightweight Triton bottoms make the "heavy look" free and easy. With a price to match. Most Pedwin styles $15 to $25.

Pedwin

Shiny polyester Nik Nik shirts.   Stretch polyester tops and pants.   Terry toweling jumpsuits.

Caught between the hippie and mod fashion extremes of the early '70s, the rest of us settled for easy-care. Whether it was casual, formal or business attire, being easy to wash and drip-dry dictated what we wore. Non-iron wool jersey knits and non-iron polyester were the material of choice for men and women throughout the '70s.

The '70s are often considered to be the decade that fashion forgot (or the decade of fashion that we would rather forget). And it's not hard to see why. Anything and everything became acceptable, no matter how outlandish or mismatched.

Here are some of our more questionable fashion decisions from the decade.

Shiny stretch
polyester jumpsuits.   Denim on denim.   Stretch knit pantsuits.   Safari suits.

John Travolta in *Saturday Night Fever*
(Paramount Pictures, 1977).

Dancer at Studio 54, New York.

And then there was disco.
It shone so brightly. It glittered so briefly.
And in a flash, it was gone.

Model wears sequined jumpsuit.

Dancers at Studio 54, New York.

Sporting silver lamé jumpsuits.

Menswear from the *J.C. Penny* Home Shopping Catalog, Winter 1973.

Also in Sports

11th Feb– Australian swimmer Shane Gould became the first woman to swim 1,500m freestyle in under 17 minutes.

31st Mar– American boxer Muhammad Ali suffered a broken jaw in a shock loss to Ken Norton over 12 rounds in San Diego.

5th Sep– West Indies played their first one-day Cricket International, losing to England by 1 wicket.

8th Sep– Margaret Court won her 24th and final Grand Slam singles title at the US Open Women's Tennis, Forest Hills, NY, beating fellow Australian Evonne Goolagong.

20th Sep– American tennis great Billy Jean King defeated Bobby Riggs in the 'Battle of the Sexes' (6-4, 6-3, 6-3) at the Houston Astrodome. An estimated ninety million people worldwide watched the live telecast.

14th Oct– American baseballer Willie Mays played his last MLB game, retiring from the New York Mets at age 42. He would be elected to the Baseball Hall of Fame in 1979, and presented with the Presidential Medal of Freedom by President Barack Obama (2015).

1st Dec– Jack Nicklaus finished at 13-under-par to win the Walt Disney World Open by 1 stroke from Mason Rudolph, making him the first golfer to reach $2 million in PGA Tour career earnings.

Technology and Medicine

3rd Apr–Martin Cooper made the world's first mobile phone call from a DynaTAC 8000X, the device he invented for Motorola.

6th Apr– NASA launched Pioneer 11 to flyby Jupiter and Saturn on a study mission. It would transmit data back to earth for 12 years before leaving the solar system.

20th Apr– Telesat Canada launched ANIK A2, the world's first commercial satellite for television, voice and data.

23rd Jun– The World Court condemned French nuclear tests in the Pacific. France ignored the ruling and continued testing nuclear bombs in the Pacific until 1996.

30th Jun– Astronomers aboard a Concorde jet prototype observed a 74-minute solar eclipse as they chased the moon's shadow across the Earth at twice the speed of sound. Five teams of scientists conducted five separate observation experiments while onboard.

26th Sep– Concorde made its first non-stop crossing of the Atlantic, flying from Washington, DC to Paris in 3 hours and 33 minutes.

1973– General Motors installed the first airbags in a fleet of Chevrolet Impalas for government use, and later the same year in the passenger side of Oldsmobile Toronados for public sale.

Other News from 1973

1st Jan– Denmark, Ireland and the UK joined the European Economic Community, increasing the number of member states from six to nine.

3rd Jan– Joe Biden was sworn-in as Senator from Delaware at age 30, just days after his wife and daughter were killed in a car accident. He took the oath at the Wilmington hospital where his two sons were recovering from the crash. Biden resigned from the Senate in 2009 to become Vice President under President Barack Obama, and in 2020 became the 46th President of the USA.

21st Feb– Libyan Arab Airlines Flight 114 veered off-course due to bad weather and equipment failure, entering Israeli controlled air-space over the Sinai Peninsula. Israeli fighter pilots shot down the plane, killing 108 civilians. Five of the passengers and crew survived.

17th Jul– Mohammed Daoud Khan seized power from his cousin King Zahir, proclaiming himself President of the new Republic of Afghanistan.

26th Mar   Six women broke through the glass ceiling at the London Stock Exchange, becoming the first female stockbrokers admitted as members in the institution's 171-year history.

Five of the six women members of the London Stock Exchange, 1973. From left: Muriel Wood, Susan Shaw, Hilary Root, Anthea Gaukroger and Audrey Geddes.

3rd May– Chicago's Sears Tower was completed, becoming the world's tallest building at 527 m (1,729 ft) high. It would hold the tallest building title for 25 years.

10th Jul– John Paul Getty III, grandson of oil tycoon J. Paul Getty, was kidnapped and held for ransom in Rome. When his family refused to pay, the kidnappers sent his father a lock of hair and one ear. He was released five months after being kidnapped. He was 16 years old at the time.

11th Sep– General Augusto Pinochet ousted Chilean President Salvador Allende in a military coup. Allende was the first elected Marxist president of a South American country.

20th Oct– The Sydney Opera House was opened by HM Queen Elizabeth II.

30th Oct– The Bosphorus Bridge opened in Istanbul, Turkey, connecting Europe to Asia for the first time.

16th Nov– US President Richard Nixon authorized construction of the Alaskan Oil Pipeline. Approval for the pipeline was fast-tracked as a result of the 1973-1974 Arab OPEC Oil Embargo.

17th Nov– Hundreds of Greek students were attacked by the military following protests against the ruling right-wing military dictatorship. 24 civilians died when tanks crashed through the gates of the Athens Polytechnic campus. Marshal Law was imposed to quell the riots.

20th Dec- Basque terrorists killed Spanish Prime Minister Admiral Luis Carrero Blanco with explosives placed under his passing car. His driver and bodyguard were killed with him.

Famous People Born in 1973

20th Jan– Queen Mathilde of Belgium.

31st Jan– Portia de Rossi, Australian actress.

4th Feb– Oscar De La Hoya, American boxer.

16th Feb– Cathy Freeman, Australian athlete.

25th Feb– Julio Iglesias, Jr., Spanish model & singer.

10th Mar– Eva Herzigova, Czech supermodel.

23rd Mar– Jason Kidd, Basketball player & coach.

26th Mar– Larry Page, American computer scientist & businessman (co-founded Google).

1st Apr– Rachel Maddow, American political analyst, radio & TV personality.

4th Apr– David Blaine, American magician & illusionist.

5th Apr– Pharrell Williams, American singer, songwriter, music producer & film producer.

14th Apr– Adrien Brody, American actor.

24th Apr– Sachin Tendulkar, Indian Cricket Batsman & captain.

20th May– Elsa [Lunghini], French singer & actress.

1st Jun– Heidi Klum, German model & TV presenter.

2nd Jun– Kevin Feige, American producer, President of Marvel Studios (2007-).

15th Jun– Neil Patrick Harris, American stage & screen actor.

14th Jul– Halil Mutlu, Bulgarian-Turkish weightlifter (Olympic & 5x World Champion).

26th Jul– Kate Beckinsale, British actress.

3rd Aug– Jay Cutler, American bodybuilder (4x Mr. Olympia winner).

14th Aug– Kieren Perkins, Australian swimmer.

22nd Aug– Kristen Wiig, American comedian & actress.

5th Sep– Rose McGowan, American actress & sexual harassment activist.

12th Sep– Paul Walker, American actor (d. 2013).

3rd Oct– Neve Campbell, Canadian actress.

22nd Oct– Ichiro Suzuki, Japanese MBL All Star baseball outfielder.

26th Oct– Seth MacFarlane, American actor, animator, TV producer & filmmaker.

1st Nov– Aishwarya Rai, Indian actress & beauty queen (Miss World 1994).

2nd Dec– Monica Seles, Yugoslavian-American tennis player.

2nd Dec– Jan Ullrich, German road cyclist.

4th Dec– Tyra Banks, American model & TV presenter.

28th Dec– Seth Meyers, American actor, comedian, writer & producer.

Harley-Davidson Z-90.
The Great American Freedom Machine.

Standard with sunroof at no extra cost.

The Harley-Davidson Z-90. Cycling's one-upmanship over convertibles.

Nothing to fence you in or hold you back. And obviously Harley-Davidson.

Two-stroke design mastery. Responsive 90cc power. Metered oil injection to end fuel mixing. Four-speed transmission.

Head turning, high-gloss fenders of gleaming stainless. Double downtube frame.

Gear up right, then grab a little freedom. A lot. Ride in style on the completely new-styled Z-90.

You deserve it.

Harley-Davidson Z-90.
The Great American Freedom Machine.

1973 in Numbers

Census Statistics [1]

- Population of the world   3.93 billion
- Population in the United States   215.18 million
- Population in the United Kingdom   56.01 million
- Population in Canada   22.42 million
- Population in Australia   13.43 million
- Average age for marriage of women   21.0 years old
- Average age for marriage of men   23.2 years old
- Average family income USA $12,050 per year
- Unemployment rate USA   4.9 %

Costs of Goods [2]

- Average new house $27,866
- Average new car $3,930
- A gallon of gasoline $0.36
- A loaf of bread $0.29
- Pork, roast $0.59 per pound
- Chicken, quartered $0.59 per pound
- Frankfurters, Grand Union $0.89 per pound
- Oranges, Valencia $0.59 for 10
- Bananas $0.14 per pound
- Lettuce, Romaine $0.39 per piece
- Soup, Campbell's $0.16 per can
- Fresh eggs $0.45 per dozen
- Razor blades, Gilette $0.65 per 5 pack
- Soap, Ivory $0.39 for 4 bars
- A cinema ticket $1.50

[1] Figures taken from worldometers.info/world-population, US National Center for Health Statistics, *Divorce and Divorce Rates* US (cdc.gov/nchs/data/series/sr_21/sr21_029.pdf) and United States Census Bureau, *Historical Marital Status Tables* (census.gov/data/tables/time-series/demo/families/marital.html).
[2] Figures from thepeoplehistory.com, mclib.info/reference/local-history & dqydj.com/historical-home-prices/.

These words first appeared in print in the year 1973.

biosecurity

cash-strapped

detox

Global Positioning System

bikini wax

LOCKDOWN

Hard disk

Food processor

triathlon

reverse engineer

Video game

STRESSED

Soccer mom

revolving-door

duct tape

Super-spreader

fact-check

* From merriam-webster.com/time-traveler/1973.

Flashback books make the perfect gift- https://bit.ly/FlashbackSeries

A heartfelt plea from the author:

I sincerely hope you enjoyed reading this book and that it brought back many fond memories from the past.

Success as an author has become increasingly difficult with the proliferation of **AI generated** copycat books by unscrupulous sellers. They are clever enough to escape copyright action and use dark web tactics to secure paid-for **fake reviews**, something I would never do.

Hence I would like to ask you — I plead with you — the reader, to leave a star rating or review on Amazon. This helps make my book discoverable for new readers, and helps me to compete fairly against the devious copycats.

If this book was a gift to you, you can leave stars or a review on your own Amazon account, or you can ask the gift-giver or a family member to do this on your behalf.

I have enjoyed researching and writing this book for you and would greatly appreciate your feedback.

Best regards,
Bernard Bradforsand-Tyler.

Please leave a
book review/rating at:

https://bit.ly/1973reviews

Or scan the QR code:

Image Attributions

Photographs and images used in this book are reproduced courtesy of the following:

Page 4 – From *National Geographic* Magazine Apr 1973. Source: vintage-ads.livejournal.com/2129105.html (PD image).*
Page 6 – Impeach Nixon protestors by Marion S. Trikosko or Thomas J. O'Halloran, 22nd Oct 1973.
Source: commons.wikimedia.org/wiki/Category:Impeachment_process_against_Richard_Nixon (PD image).
Page 7 – Summer Jam Rock Festival, July 1973. Creator unknown. Source: vintag.es/2014/10/pictures-of-fans-at-1973-summer-jam.html. Pre-1978, no copyright mark (PD image). – Publicity image of The Loud family from *An American Family* by PBS. Source: en.wikipedia.org/wiki/An_American_Family (PD image).
Page 8 – From *Playboy* Magazine Dec 1973 (PD image).*
Page 9 – College girls in 1973 by Ed Uthman. Source: en.wikipedia.org/wiki/Youth#/media/File:1970sgirls.jpg. Attribution CC BY-SA 2.0. – University of Western Florida outdoor class in 1976. Source: uwfphotos.smugmug.com/Historical-Photos/Student-Life/i-qBD8HcW.
Page 10 – Boys on a street, and Shaftsbury Avenue in 1973, unknown creators. Sources: flashbak.com/an-utterly-different-city-london-in-1973-424081/. Pre-1978, no copyright mark (PD image).
Page 11 – The Grill Pub stormed, by *The Scotsman* newspaper. 20th Apr 1973. Source: scotsman.com/arts-and-culture/women-who-stormed-men-only-pub-1973-258644. – Boy crossing road, date and creator unknown. Both images this page are pre-1978, no copyright mark (PD image).
Page 12 – 1973 Converse print advert. Source: ebay.com (PD image).*
Page 13– UK Second Gay Pride march, 1973, creator unknown. Source: bishopsgate.org.uk/stories/gallery-the-gay-liberation-front-the-origins-of-pride. Pre-1978, no copyright mark (PD image). – Engineers strike, 1973, creator unknown. Pre-1978, no copyright mark (PD image).
Page 14 – Commune members, source: allthatsinteresting.com/hippie-communes. – Commune members pose in front of a tipi, by John Olson from Life Magazine, 18th Jul 1969. Source: books.google.com/books?id=K08EAAAAMBAJ&printsec.
Page 15 – Tending to the fields, source: burlingtonfreepress.com/story/news/local/vermont/2015/07/24/vermont-remains-hippie-epicenter/30564907/, photo by Rebecca Lepkoff of Vermont Historical Society. – Geodesic dome, source: vpr.org/post/communes-hippie-invasion-and-how-1970s-changed-state#stream/0 by Kate Daloz. – Commune bus, source: allthatsinteresting.com/hippie-communes. All images this page are pre-1978, no copyright mark (PD image).
Page 16 – Thunderbird print advert from *Hot Rod Magazine* April 1973. Source: classiccarstodayonline.com/classic-car-print-advertisements/ (PD image).*
Page 17 – Friday afternoon traffic heading out of Atlanta, by Al Stephenson / AJC file. Source: ajc.com/lifestyles/flashback-photos-through-the-years-1951-1997/ByK7dbup2R66nM4TMIWX9O/.
– Valley View Mall aerial photo, creator unknown. Pre-1978, no copyright mark (PD image).
Page 18 – 1973 Chrysler Plymouth from *Playboy* magazine May 1973. – 1973 Oldsmoble Cutlass Salon print advertisment, source unknown. – 1973 AMC Hornet from *Playboy* magazine. All items pre-1978, no copyright mark (PD image).
Page 19 – 1973 Porshe 914 print ad from *Newsweek* 16th Apr1973, posted by SenseiAlan. Source: flickr.com/photos/91591049@N00/17056063464/in/dateposted/ Attribution 2.0 Generic (CC BY 2.0). – 1973 Datsun 610 print ad from *Playboy* magazine Feb 1973. Source: flickr.com/photos/31411679@N08/6249891453 posted by Alden Jewell. Attribution 4.0 International (CC BY 4.0). – 1973 BMW Beetle print advertisement, source unknown.
Page 20 – From *Vintage Life* Magazine, 17th Nov 1972. source: oldcarandtruckads.com. (PD image).*
Page 21 – 1973 Chevolet advert. Source: classiccarstodayonline.com/classic-car-print-advertisements/. (PD image).*
Page 22 – Signing of the Paris Peace Accords by Knudsen, Robert L. (Robert LeRoy). Source: commons.wikimedia.org/wiki/File:Vietnam_peace_agreement_signing.jpg (PD image). – The signed document, picture taken at the National Air and Space Museum's Steven F. Udvar-Hazy Center in Chantilly, Virginia, USA. by Sanjay Acharya.
Source: en.wikipedia.org/wiki/Paris_Peace_Accords. Attribution-ShareAlike 4.0 International (CC BY-SA 4.0).
Page 23 – American POWs assembling, by Werner Schulze. Source: flickr.com/photos/13476480@N07/51510294726.
– POWs flying home, source: commons.wikimedia.org/wiki/File:BR,_Vietnam,_1973,_POW_Homecoming,_file_04.jpg. Images this page were taken as works of the US federal government, and are in the public domain.
Page 24 – 1973 TWA print advert. Source: ebay.com (PD image).*
Page 25 – Newspaper articles from the 1970s and movie posters by Warner Bros. and 20th Century Fox. (PD images).**
Page 26 – From *Time* magazine, 26th Mar 1973 posted by SenseiAlan. Source: flickr.com/photos/91591049@N00/26543346392. Attribution 2.0 Generic (CC BY 2.0)
Page 27 – *Operation Crossroads*, Bikini Atoll, 25th July 1946. Source: en.wikipedia.org/wiki/Operation_Crossroads.
– *Small Boy* at Nevada Proving Grounds, 14th July 1962. Source: commons.wikimedia.org/wiki/File:Small_Boy_nuclear_test_1962.jpg. All photos this page by either US Army or Navy and are in the public domain. (PD images).
Page 28 – Egyptian forces cross the Suez Canal, from *Military Battles on the Egyptian Front* by Gammal Hammad. Published by Dār al-Shurūq, Egypt. Source: https://en.wikipedia.org/wiki/Operation_Badr_(1973) (PD image). – Israeli soldiers by the Israel Defense Forces. Source: commons.wikimedia.org/wiki/Category:Yom_Kippur_War (PD image).
Page 29 – Speed limit and No Gas station, creators unknown. Source: commons.wikimedia.org/wiki/Category:Gas_shortage_of_1973_in_the_United_States. Images this page are pre-1978, no copyright mark (PD images).
Page 30 – 1973 Encyclopaedia Britannica print advert. Source: ebay.com (PD image).*
Page 31 – From *Sports Illustrated* Magazine 14th May 1973. Source: ebay.com (PD image).*
Page 32 – Republican arrests, creators unknown. Source: anphoblacht.com/contents/26282. Pre-1978, no copyright mark (PD images). – Peace Wall by Robin Kirk, 2008. Source: flickr.com/photos/rightsatduke/4595426547/. Attribution 4.0 International (CC BY 4.0).
Page 33 – Mainland Campaign, London 1974, creator unknown. – Bloody Sunday riots, creator unknown. Source: thetimes.co.uk/article/bloody-sunday-paratrooper-fired-as-if-on-turkey-shoot-2klcfqhqz. Pre-1978, no mark (PD images).
Page 35 – 1973 Banquet Frozen Food print advert. Source: ebay.com (PD image).*
Page 36 – 1973 General Electric camera FlashBar print advert. Source: ebay.com (PD image).*
Page 37 – Norma McCorvey attributed to Lorie Shaull. Source: en.wikipedia.org/wiki/Norma_McCorvey (PD image).*
– Street march in 1973, creator unknown. Source: nzhistory.govt.nz/media/photo/pro-abortion-march-1973 (PD image).*
Page 38 – Operation Wounded Knee, creator unknown. Source: libcom.org/article/siege-wounded-knee-1973. Pre-1978, no copyright mark (PD image). – Sacheen Littlefeather at the 45th Academy Awards. Source: en.wikipedia.org/wiki/Sacheen_Littlefeather. Attribution 2.0 Generic (CC BY 2.0).
Page 39 – Nixon signs ESA, creator unknown, 28th Dec 1973. Source: www.politico.com/story/2012/12/this-day-in-politics-085535. – Bald eagle and Gray wolf from USFWS Endangered Species, creators unknown. Sources: en.wikipedia.org/wiki/Bald_eagle#/media/File:About_to_Launch_(26075320352).jpg and commons.wikimedia.org/wiki/File:Endangered_gray_wolf_%28Canis_lupus%29.jpg (PD images).*
Page 40 – 1973 Sony portable TV print advert. Source: ebay.com (PD image).*
Page 41 – *All in the Family* screen still, 4th May 1971, by CBS Television.** Source: en.wikipedia.org/wiki/All_in_the_Family#/media/File: Archie_and_Lionel_All_in_the_Family_1971.JPG.
Page 42 – *The Mary Tyler Moore Show* publicity image by CBS, 1970.** Source: commons.wikimedia.org/wiki/File:Mary_Tyler_Moore_cast_1970_1977.JPG. (PD image). – Still image and poster from the TV series *Hawaii Five-O* by CBS, 1970.**

Page 43 – Screen still from *The Young and The Restless* by Bell Dramatic Serial & Corday, 1973.** – Screen still from *Kojak* by Universal Television, 1973.** – Publicity photo of Lee Majors from *The Six Million Dollar Man,* 17th Nov 1973. Source: commons.wikimedia.org/wiki/File:Six_million_dollar_man_1973.JPG. – Screen still from *Police Story* by NBC, 1973.**
Page 44 – From *Playboy* Magazine Oct 1973. Source: ebay.com (PD image).*
Page 45 – Publicity still for *The Exorcist* by Warner Bros, 1974. Source: commons.wikimedia.org/wiki/Category:The_Exorcist _(film) (PD image).* Lee at Phoenix Comicon, 2014. Source: commons.wikimedia.org/wiki/Category:Stan_Lee (PD image).*
Page 46 – Film posters for the movies *American Graffiti* and *The Sting* by Universal Pictures.** *Papillon* by Allied Artists.**
Page 47 – Film posters for the movies *The Poseidon Adventure* by 20th Century Fox, 1972.** – *The Towering Inferno* by 20th Century Fox, Warner Bros, 1974.** – *Earthquake* by Universal Pictures, 1974.** – *Tidal Wave* by Toho Company, 1973.**
Page 48 – Photo from *The Rocky Horror Show*, German stage show 2005,** – Film poster by 20th Century Fox,** 1975.
Page 49 – From *Playboy* Magazine Dec 1973. Source: ebay.com (PD image).*
Page 50 – Pink Floyd, circa 1973, creator unknown. – Bruce Springsteen live at Max's Kansas City, 31st Jan 1973, creator unknown. – Aerosmith, creator and date unknown. Photos this page are pre-1978, no copyright marks (PD images).
Page 51 – Elton in Hamburg, Germany, Mar 1972. Source: commons.wikimedia.org/wiki/Category:Elton_John_in_1972. Permission CC BY-SA 2.0. – Trade ad by Warner Bros. Records for Alice Cooper's *No More Mr. Nice Guy,* from Billboard 31st Mar 1973. Source- commons.wikimedia.org/wiki/File:Alice_Cooper_-_No_More_Mr._Nice_Guy_%281973%29.jpg.
– Marvin Gaye by MoTown Records. – Stevie Wonder by MoTown Records, 21st Aug 1973. Source: commons.wikimedia. org/wiki/Category:Stevie_wonder_in_1973. Photos this page are pre-1978, no copyright marks (PD images).
Page 52 – Roberta Flack by Atlantic Records, 1976. Source: commons.wikimedia.org/wiki/Category:Roberta_Flack.
– Kristofferson publicity photo by Magna Artists, 1978. Source: commons.wikimedia.org/wiki/Category:Kris_Kristofferson.
– Diana Ross for Mowtown Records, 22nd Aug 1976. Source: commons.wikimedia.org/wiki/Category:Diana_Ross_in_the_ 1970s. – Cher from the TV special *Entertainer of the Year*, 27th Dec 1973. Source: commons. wikimedia.org/wiki/Category: Cher_(singer)_in_1973. All photos this page are pre-1978, no copyright marks (PD images).
Page 53 – Elton John from *The Cher Show*, CBS Television. Source: commons.wikimedia.org/wiki/Category:Elton_John_ in_1975. – Carly Simon publicity photo for Elektra. Source: commons.wikimedia.org/wiki/Category:Carly_Simon. Photos this page are pre-1978, no copyright marks (PD images).
Page 54 – From *Sports Illustrated* Magazine 23rd Apr 1973. Source: ebay.com (PD image).*
Page 55 – 1973 Panasonic car stereo print advert. Source: ebay.com (PD image).*
Page 56 – Pants and skirt-suit, 1969, creator unknown. Pre-1978, (PD image). – Maxi-dress by YSL, Spring-Summer 1969. Source: minniemuse.com/articles/creative-connections/ patchwork. Pre-1978, (PD image).
Page 57 – Elizabeth Taylor, source: instyle.com/celebrity/transformations/elizabeth-taylors-changing-looks. – Thea Porter dress, photographer Patrick Hunt, 1970. – Weipert and Burda fashion show, Apr 1972, photo by Friedrich Magnussen. Permission CC BY-SA 3.0 DE. – Mini dresses, sources: pinterest.com/pin/9978247967669796/ and retrospace.org/2011_01_01_archive.html unknown photographers. Pre-1978, no copyright mark (PD image).
Page 58 – Fashions from Sears Catalogues, Pre-1978, no copyright mark (PD image). – Hungarian singer Szűcs Judit wears embroidered demin. Source: commons.wikimedia.org/wiki/File:Szűcs_Judit_énekesnő._Fortepan_88657.jpg. Licensed under the Creative Commons Attribution-Share Alike 3.0 Unported. – Knit polyester pants from the 1975 J.C. Penney catalog. Pre-1978, no copyright marks (PD image). – Flared jumpsuits, creator unknown. Pre-1978, no marks (PD image).
Page 59 – From *Playboy* Sep 1973, posted by SenseiAlan. Source: flickr.com/photos/91591049@N00/24977545265/. Attribution 2.0 Generic (CC BY 2.0).
Page 60 – Nik Nik shirts, polyester jumpsuits, and knit pantsuits, source: onedio.com/haber/erkekte-retro-modasinin-tutmamasinin-32-mantikli-sebebi-300983. – Polyester tops and pants, toweling jumpsuits, and shrink tops by Colombia Minerva, source: flashbak.com/the-good-the-bad-and-the-tacky-20-fashion-trends-of-the-1970s-26213/. – Denim on denim source: typesofjeanfits.com/a-brief-history-of-jeans-denim-history-timeline/. – Safari suits source: klyker.com/ 1970s-fashion/. All images this page Pre-1978, no copyright mark or renewal (PD image).
Page 61 – Still image from the film *Saturday Night Fever* by Paramount Pictures.** Source: vocal.media/beat/the-list-saturday-night-fever-40th-anniversary. – Dancers Studio 54, sources: definition.org/studio-54/2/ & alexilubomirski.com/image-collections/studio-54. Pre-1978, no copyright marks (PD image).
Page 62 – *From J.C. Penny Home Shopping Catalog* Winter 1973 (PD image).*
Page 63 – King in 2016, by Jonathan Exley. Source: commons.wikimedia.org/wiki/Category:Billie_Jean_King. Pre-1978 (PD image). – Willie Mays by William C. Greene. Source: commons.wikimedia.org/wiki/Category:Willie_Mays (PD image).
– Jack Nicklaus, creator unknown. Source: prosportsmemorabilia.com. Pre-1978 (PD image).
Page 64 – From *National Geographic* Mag Apr 1973 (PD image).*
Page 65 – Motorola DynaTAC 8000x, creator unknown. Pre-1978 (PD image). – Artist impression *Pioneer 11* by Rick Guidice, Source: nasa.gov/feature/40-years-ago-pioneer-11-first-to-explore-saturn (PD image). – Concorde in flight, creator unknown. Pre-1978 (PD image).
Page 66 – Joseph Biden official Presidential portrait, 2nd March 2021. Source: commons.wikimedia.org/wiki/ Joe_Biden (PD image). – First women of the London Stock Exchange by Kenneth Mason for The Daily Telegraph. Source: telegraph.co.uk/multimedia/archive/02519/london_2519350k.jpg. This image is reproduced under USA Fair Use laws due to: 1- image is a low resolution copy; 2- image does not devalue the ability of the copyright holder to profit from the original work; 3- The image is relevant to the article created and is too small to make illegal copies for use in another book – Sears Tower photo by Balthazar Korab, 1974. Source: loc.gov/item/2021636626/ (PD image).
Page 67– Sydney Opera House, creator unknown. – Alaskan Oil Pipeline by Margaret Kriz Hobson for E&E News.
– PM Blanco by Gianni Cattaneo. Source: en.wikipedia.org/wiki/File:Luis_Carrero_Blanco.jpg. All images this page are pre-1978, no copyright mark (PD images).
Page 68 & 69 – All photos are, where possible, CC BY 2.0 or PD images made available by the creator for free use including commercial use. Where commercial use photos are unavailable, photos are included here for information only under US fair use laws due to: 1- images are low resolution copies; 2- images do not devalue the ability of the copyright holders to profit from the original works in any way; 3- Images are too small to be used to make illegal copies for use in another book; 4- The images are relevant to the article created.
Page 70 – From *Hot Rod* Magazine Feb 1973. Source: ebay (PD image).*

*Advertisement (or image from an advertisement) is in the public domain because it was published in a collective work (such as a periodical issue) in the US between 1925 and 1977 and without a copyright notice specific to the advertisement. **Posters for movies or events are either in the public domain (published in the US between 1925 and 1977 and without a copyright notice specific to the artwork) or owned by the production company, creator, or distributor of the movie or event. Posters, where not in the public domain, and screen stills from movies or TV shows, are reproduced here under USA Fair Use laws due to: 1- images are low resolution copies; 2- images do not devalue the ability of the copyright holders to profit from the original works in any way; 3- Images are too small to be used to make illegal copies for use in another book; 4- The images are relevant to the article created.

Printed in Poland
by Amazon Fulfillment
Poland Sp. z o.o., Wrocław

26592158R10043